PROFIT AND LOSS:

THE HIGH COST OF COMPLAINING

AND OTHER UNPROFESSIONAL CONDUCT

BY J. LEWIS, M.ED., BAMS, CDS

PREFACE BY WILLIAM R. FOLDS, JR.
FOREWORD BY JASON KREIDER

Assumptions the complainer makes when they begin speaking negatively:

(1) The complainer assumes that the person or group listening to their complaints actually wants to hear their statements.

This assumption usually transcends professionalism, character, and personal desire. The complainer chooses to make an unprofessional move and force his/her audience into listening.

(2) The complainer assumes that their issue or issues is/are more important than anything else their audience has going on at the time. I'll develop this later, but a quick example is someone complaining about being tired to someone who just lost their mother. Obviously, the fatigue issue pales in comparison to a death in the family.

(3) The complainer assumes that there is nothing more important to do at the time, be it work or personal tasks, that outweigh the significance of voicing the complaint.

This is the book that we all needed twenty or thirty years ago. Our work ethic has changed, and we as Americans have turned into whiny sissies who complain constantly. I honestly don't believe that employers and employees realize how common this detraction from productivity and profit really is.

This book serves several purposes – first to make people aware of this annoying, unhealthy habit or group of habits; secondly, to address the issues in the workplace and in our personal lives, and lastly, to develop healthier, more rewarding behaviors that will allow us all more success.

Copyright 2016

All rights reserved. EBooks are not transferable and cannot be given away, sold, or shared. Without limiting the rights under copyright reserved above, no part of this publication may be reproduced, stored in, or introduced into a retrieval system or transmitted, in any form or by any means (electronic, mechanical, photocopying, recording, or otherwise), without the prior written permission of the owner.

The scanning, uploading, and distribution of this book via the Internet or any other means without the permission of the owner is illegal and punishable by law. Please purchase only authorized electronic editions, and do not participate in or encourage electronic piracy of copyrighted materials. Your support of the author's rights is appreciated.

PREFACE

I worked with James in several capacities, first when I was a mid-level Non-Commissioned Officer (NCO) and he was a fairly new airman, and I was in charge of our police flight. He had the typical wild and wooly times as par the course for a 19-year-old, but he was always a straight shooter. We later worked together as NCOs on the commander's staff.

I could always count on James to be honest, strongly straightforward, at times to the point of pushing the envelope, but never wavering. He admitted and owned up to mistakes, corrected problems, and established a great baseline for credibility through the entire unit, and eventually the base.

I watched him and his motivation and a death-grip on advancement through the years, and he learned that the only true way to get ahead while taking care of his supervisors and subordinates alike was to be honest, hold nothing back, and even be a little rough and abrupt. There was never a concern as to where he stood on a policy or issue, or where people stood with him.

With that said, if you are a business owner or manager, and your people are being less than productive, and they're complaining, whining and wasting time, I'd suggest a guy like James to break it down for you, tell you what you need to look for, how to identify the various behaviors, and ultimately, how to fix it.

William R. Folds, Jr.
United States Air Force Retired
Veterans Administration Retired

FOREWORD

Author James Lewis has been in an incredible variety of positions over his forty-plus years in the work force, starting at age ten with a successful car detailing business, moving to lawn mowing, and attaining his first W-2 position at a Western Auto store in 1977.

He attained a Master's in Education, a Bachelor's of Applied Medical Science in Sociology/Psychology, and a Bachelor's of Applied Science in Criminal Justice, all through the University of Maryland, and all completed while in the Air Force and Air Force Reserve.

His bright attitude, quick wit, and sometimes sarcastic demeanor allows him to inject humor and address serious personality and professionalism issues in the workplace and in public while avoiding direct lecturing or condescension.

In the legal field, he has worked as an expert witness in automotive lemon law and trucking/towing liability cases, with over 10,000 written opinions, more than 800 court appearances, and 165 depositions. His constant presence in the public domain has allowed him to be a strong voice in the community, giving advice and direction on a number of subjects.

He is an accomplished published author with self-help, documentary, and action/adventure fiction books. He now turns his attention to a series of management and leadership guides, the first on Profit and Loss: The High Cost of Complaining, showing managers and business owners just how they can become more profitable and have happier customers and employees by using several methods to limit or eliminate negative attitudes in the workplace.

Jason Kreider

DISCLAIMER: I am not a politically correct person. With that said, I don't curse or threaten in order to pursue personal enjoyment. I've told these stories, though, exactly as they played out so my readers can see the language used by people who could be YOUR employees, and the response their actions and words illicit in me.

If you are offended by an occasional bad word, I should suggest that this is reality and how many regular people talk. I should also suggest that you lower your sensitivity level, since you may not get much worked out without having some boldness and gumption under your belt.

We Americans are a spoiled, whiny bunch. I spent a year in Korea, and the Koreans are some of the hardest working people I've ever seen. I recall seeing an eighty or ninety-year-old man walking along a road, with a large sack of rice on his back – it had to weigh near a hundred pounds, which was about what he weighed. As I passed on my bicycle, he smiled and greeted me in Korean. I returned the greeting and smile, immediately thinking of how some Americans of young working age would be pitching a fit if they had to manually carry a bag like that and didn't have transportation.

It seems that most Americans aren't happy unless they're whining, or at least have something to whine about. If you take away the issue, or solve their problem, many people are truly lost that they can't use complaining as a method to get attention. Pretty pathetic since 95% of my subjects involve ADULTS.

Pull up your underdrawers and let's get to work!

J. Lewis

Formal Complaints versus Complaining to Whine

When I first ran the idea for this book past several friends, a couple of them said I couldn't stop people from having legitimate complaints. And of course I can't, and that's 180 degrees opposite of my intentions.

It is mandatory for business success, I believe, to have a process where an employee can air a grievance. I'm also not talking about real complaints about workplace issues in the title of this book, but the unproductive, unprofessional versions that costs employers millions of dollars each year.

I strongly believe that a formal program should be in place in each organization and sub-organization, a chain of command (or term of your choosing) should be in place and well-advertised, and the method for airing complaints should be fully addressed. This should be done in a company handbook, as well as mentioned in new hire orientation or where employees are transferred in from another section of division.

Several thoughts come to mind that may help you formulate this formal process or tune-up the current process, which ever may apply to your situation.

Human Resources is NOT the "complaint department." At least it shouldn't be. For example, a person who works in a warehouse selecting freight for transportation orders and loading trucks has a first-line supervisor. That first-line supervisor likely has a shipping and receiving manager. That manager reports to an operations manager. That operations manager reports to a vice president or business owner.

If the person who operates a forklift, selecting orders and loading trucks, has a problem and goes straight to Human Resources, there are four supervisors who have now been disrespected and unused, as designed by the business owner. This is an easy cause for hard feelings and resentment, and the entry-level employee would have just thrown everyone in their chain of command "under the bus." Under the bus is a place that no one wants to be. First, when attention comes from the top down after HR makes their notification of an existing problem, everyone in that chain is caught off-guard, surprised, and embarrassed. These elements and feelings aren't productive for getting a job done or a complaint resolved.

Ideally, the order picker should go to their first-line supervisor and report their issue. This courtesy goes a long way in total section morale and comradery. If the issue is one that requires a higher pay grade, so to speak, than that of the first-line supervisor, the supervisor can walk the employee to their manager, and so on until the problem is resolved.

Many, many companies misuse their HR person or department. The only time I'd recommend going straight to HR and bypassing the chain of command is in the case of very serious allegations, like sexual harassment or threats of violence, Other routine complaints NEED to be handled through the chain of command, since it is those very people who would be resolving any operations-related issue, not HR.

One of my first supervisors taught me a valuable lesson. He said he'd gladly talk to me about anything anytime. However, comma, and that's a big comma...if you're coming into his office with a complaint, make sure you have a solution in your back pocket. Complaint...idea...and his help with resolution...that's how things can be handled. If you're just coming in with a complaint and haven't taken the time to figure out how to fix the problem and make a suggestion...you're just whining.

Let's Agree

I want to lay a few things out that may give away quite a lot about my personality, and that's just fine. I'm hoping it will also bring us to common ground on our feelings about the activities I'll be explaining and expanding on.

I'm a very no-nonsense sort of guy, yet when I manage, I do so with a Laissez-Faire attitude. I believe that once your employees are made aware of your expectations, fully understand their jobs and procedures, are fully indoctrinated on your company's checklists, policies, or habits, you should be able to go to a "hands off" management style. Many managers want to look over a person's shoulder, and many employees require that level of supervision. It's your choice as a manager whether you want to keep a grown adult on your staff who requires constant hand-holding and upkeep.

I'm very strict, but don't do the "prison guard walk" in the work section to make sure everyone has their nose to the grindstone. Ultimately, I want to be happy with my new hires, pleased with the progress and understanding I've had with current employees, and have those who are on probation or a short leash in full knowledge of their situation and fragile existence in the workplace.

Agree with me please that revenue is revenue. Whether we're talking lost sales, lost marketing opportunities, or wasted wages, it's still money lost off the bottom line calculated at the end of the year. Revenue is revenue.

Agree with me please that most conflicts, "dropped balls," missed deadlines, and other work failures occur because proper communication wasn't maintained.

Agree with me please that it is your responsibility as a manager or business owner to initiate communication and maintain it at all times. (Works wonders to avoid surprises versus that ONE-time communication during an annual review)

Agree with me please that all employees are accountable for their behavior and performance while at work and while earning wages.

Agree with me please that the first thing an irresponsible person does when caught being irresponsible is to blame others for their behavior.

Agree with me please that it is the responsibility of the manager or owner to provide a safe workplace, and one that is free of harassment or discrimination; and that you jump immediately to rectify problems noted in these areas.

Agree with me please that complaining without offering a resolution is just whining.

Agree with me please that gossiping wastes wages, hurts productivity, damages morale, and is wholly unprofessional.

Agree with me please that bitching, whining, moaning, groaning, kicking rocks, or crying can all be categorized under the header "complaining"...all for the general discussion in this book. Please understand that no matter how we interpret or label a given negative behavior, it is all damaging and unproductive.

Agree with me please that you don't like to hear people constantly talking in a negative manner.

Because of that, agree with me please that anyone who shares your attitude about complaining and whining may look for another job if they get tired of hearing it from other employees.

And then you've lost a GOOD employee because of some bad ones, and you're going the wrong way on the production and success portions of your career. Agree with me?

Complainer Profile

As I explained, I chose the term "complaining" to head up a large group of verbal negative behavior methods, simply because most of what I'm going to address deals with complaining in some form or another. There are several other verbal methods with which a person can exude a negative attitude, and we can draw a larger picture with the terms bitching, whining, and complaining.

Before we press into actual scenarios and remedies, let's establish what complaining is, at least in the category(s) that I'm addressing.

Complaining is negative speech from one person to another, or it can take written or electronic form. There are many facets to the initial complaining action, and even more divisions and tangents after the words are expressed. In the scenarios I draw out, you'll notice quite a few tangents that this communication can take, each with a significant impact on the individuals involved.

I'll be referring to these "complaining qualifiers" throughout this publication, and will ask you to look back at these statements as we explore more detailed developments.

Complaining qualifiers – items that the complainer assumes when they began speaking negatively. They are:

(1) The complainer assumes that the person or group listening to their complaints actually wants to hear their statements.

This assumption usually transcends professionalism, character, and personal desire. The complainer chooses to make an unprofessional move and force his/her audience into listening.

(2) The complainer assumes that their issue or issues is/are more important than anything else the audience has going on at the time.

(3) The complainer assumes that there is nothing more important to do at the time, be it work or personal tasks, that outweigh the significance of voicing the complaint.

Throughout this guide, I'll be drawing and explaining scenarios I've experienced, and then explain the numerous tangents developed after the initial complaint or attitude. These include customer perception, fellow employee perception, business owner observations, and financial impact.

Many of my scenarios involve retail experiences. I've traveled for work for many years, and deal with fast food employees, those working in service stations, trucks stops, and "sit-down" restaurants. By no means are these scenarios limited to these customer service positions. The same rules apply to warehouse workers, folks in an auto parts store, an insurance agency or lawfirm.

Let's go over the general properties of the complainer themselves. Please understand that these are generalizations, and you as a business owner, manager, or employee are encouraged to survey and determine for yourself exactly what you're dealing with in the people you contact.

Emotionally weak – despite at times being loud and demanding of you to hear their complaints, most people who complain regularly, or as a matter of constant conversation (more later), are very emotionally weak. This weakness can be attributed to several factors: the person has never had serious responsibility, thus never "grew up"; the person has never been a supervisor and had to deal with the drama and repercussions caused by someone like themselves; the person simply stopped maturing, either at the point of a drastic incident or event, or just when they decided to quit taking responsibility for their actions, or were no longer challenged for accountability.

Most complainers are very insecure in their positions, insecure in their manhood or womanhood, and their only successful way of being assertive or proactive is to be negative and complain or whine.

It is often that you have grown adults who whine, complain, and throw temper tantrums, always walking around with a chip on their shoulder – I call them "Forty-year-old adolescents."

Pettiness – being petty takes many forms. People who you may not expect to act this way may surprise you by becoming exceptionally trivial and picky about minor details, a facet of being petty. Ignorance on a particular subject or in general, arrogance, and a lack of maturity can all lead to the end result of petty behavior.

The competitor – many of us have seen this guy or girl. One person whines that they had to work two hours of overtime last week, and this person jumps in, claiming that they had to work four hours. I'll give you a way to handle work-related objections and complaints in a few chapters.

The one-upper – this person is like the competitor, although while the competitor may be slightly reasonable, the one-upper has to go to outlandish lengths to make sure another person can't get close to competing with them. Usually causes huge amounts of tension and anguish in the work environment.

The game of one-upmanship is a conscious struggle for psychological superiority, often employing passive - aggressive behavior to specifically demoralize or dis-empower the thinking subject, making the aggressor look more knowledgeable, or having experienced more.

The know-it-all – while this person may not be particularly good at their job, or punctual, or professional, you'd never know it according to them. They have to be in charge at every occasion, making sure to boast that they know more about a job or task than others present. This is guided by strong insecurities, and can be addressed fairly easily.

The know-it-all is usually a person who constantly presents their input as though they were professionally trained, schooled, or have firsthand insight into subjects when it is evident this is not the case. Opinions, suggestions, thoughts, and commentary from everyone else is quickly shot down as incorrect, nonsensical, and disruptive

The problem with the know-it-all is two-fold: if allowed to run things like they want, they'll anger and alienate your entire crew and disrespect your position, usually indicating that they don't need supervision; if corrected, they'll throw a temper tantrum and cause work interruptions.

Not my job – this person studied their job description with a magnifying glass and balks at any mention of helping someone with a joint task or team project, because it's not their job or in their job description. This type of person has little pride or honor, and has no problem watching a pregnant lady take out a heavy garbage can when they could have easily pitched in and helped out of courtesy. Ironically, this person is also the one to scream the loudest when they don't get a huge raise or a promotion, since their do "their job" so well. The problem is that is all they'll do is what is on an outline of duties.

The interrupter – the impact seen because of this person seems obvious, but it isn't. It is good to encourage "visiting" sessions during slow times at work, as many people pick up valuable training and information in a casual environment, and you can utilize your experienced people in this capacity. The interrupter always jumps the gun and has to be the center of attention, and the most important person on hand. The smartest person in the room, as it were.

They'll interrupt someone's story or account with "That's nothing, check out what happened to me." In other words, what the first just said is worthless, means nothing, but what I'm going to tell you now is worth listening to. Even the most courteous and patient employee will stop talking and participating after a couple of these interruptions.

The interrupter loves to hear themselves talk. No one's account of an incident is as good or accurate as theirs. They'll step on someone just to get their version in so the crowd can hear it.

The interrupter usually complains the loudest, and because they step on other's words, their complaints ring the clearest.

The whiner – this one appears harmless, but can cause a manager or supervisor the most stress. A new schedule will be posted, or a change in work rules, and people will talk about it in a group. This person usually stays behind after a meeting to go directly to the manager or supervisor for *their* version of why this or that won't work.

They usually have an actual whine to their voice, and wear their feelings on their sleeves. If you dismiss them, don't hear them out fully, or don't address their concern(s), they'll take it very personally…producing pouting, sullenness, anger, tantrums, or worse. We should agree that none of these emotions being displayed in a workplace is a mature response and has any right being shown in a professional environment.

Complaining as a dialect or language – I've had many experiences where people complain in every single sentence they formulate. There's always something negative in response to anything you ask or offer as a statement. I've tried to "take them out at the knees" and remove the concept of complaining, as in telling them to give me something positive and they seriously can't speak. They've tuned their brains so strongly to complain constantly, it's actually become a dialect variance of the primary language, and they can't communicate without being negative. I'll say now that this is the person you want OUT of your workplace, as they spread negativity and cost you good employees.

Sandwich shop in Weatherford, Texas

On a nice Saturday in October 2013, I was off duty from my training position and my wife and I were having a great day running errands around town. We'd already done the obligatory visits to Wal-Mart, the pet store, and a bakery for a formal cake order. We decided to grab lunch before it got too late in the day. We were going to have folks over for a bar-b-q later that evening, and opted for sandwiches. We stopped at a popular sandwich chain (in Texas, at least), walked inside, and stared at the overhead menu for a moment.

We received no greeting from anyone. There was a young man at the counter, just standing there, waiting for someone to approach. The manager was disheveled, his shirt wrinkled, his face needing a shave for the past week, and his hair looking like he'd just got out of bed. Two other employees were working in the back as the manager ran the drive-thru window and tried to coordinate orders.

We quickly decided what we wanted, and stepped forward. The young man still remained silent, and had a look on his face like our presence was annoying to him. He didn't ask for our order, greet us, nothing. Very strange, I thought.

Me: "Hey, how's it going?"
Young guy: "Could be better. Can't wait 'til four o'clock."

Me: "What happens at four?"
Young guy: "I get to get the hell out of here."
(I was in a rare speechless moment)
Young guy: "Y'all figure out what you want?"

(There was another couple who had walked in behind us, and I motioned for them to take our place at the counter, and I told the young guy "Just a minute.")

My wife and I whispered back and forth, and decided to go somewhere else. I was going to speak to the manager, but figured that he knew of his young man's attitude, and was either ineffective in correcting it, or apathetic.

The young guy didn't say anything else to us, and we walked out.

Some questions which may be considered rhetorical, but as an outside observer, I'd think people would ask:

How many times per day has this happened where this guy verbalized a negative attitude about his job, time he had left on shift, or just general disdain for his position?

My wife and I had planned to order meal packages with sandwiches, chips and a drink. Our ticket would have been around eighteen dollars.

If this happens only once or twice per day, how much money do you think that franchise is losing because of this guy's negative attitude? Two lost sales at $18 is $36 per day, and possibly $252.00 per week. That's if only two customers decide against eating there. You also have to factor in the number of customers who left and would never come back. These same people will also talk to their neighbors, friends, family, coworkers, hobby club members…and how much business would these discussions cost?

I believe it is very safe to say that this guy is costing his franchisee at least $1,000 a month in lost business, plus the extension factor of all the people THOSE customers spoke to about the incidents.

I thought the incident was significant enough to play a large role in the motivation for writing this book.

Rainbows and Unicorns

A good friend of mine, a man I served with in the Air Force and have known for over thirty years, would whine occasionally when he'd call me.

I chastised him playfully about bitching and whining to me, knowing that I have a world of respect for the guy after serving at a European base with him, dealing with Communist and Labor Party strikes that effectively blockaded our base. We also served a remote tour at the same base in Korea, but a few years apart. That was considered the hardest assignment in the Air Force.

He'd call me after that and joke about "Rainbows and Unicorns", and not ever mentioning anything negative, and staying positive.

I realize that not everything in life shows you the total happiness of Rainbows and Unicorns in some magical manner. Life is life. We have negative things happen. Flat tires. Car accidents. Broken legs.

My point is instead of immediately resorting to negative words, and the obligatory bitching, whining, and complaining, first consider what you're getting ready to do the attitude and mentality of the person you're getting ready to call or speak with (in person). You can still tell your friend about a particularly difficult situation you're dealing with, but you can form your words and sentences in a manner that doesn't sound like a whiny little kid.

Greetings

Many of my peers have laughed at me because I'll adopt and stick with a phrase I like, even though it may not be politically correct or "soft" enough to fit everyone's feelings.

"Take their knees out" or "take them out at the knees" are phrases like that. I agree that they sound very harsh, but my usage is different than the imaginary action of whacking someone in the knees with a baseball bat. My definition and use deals with taking away the opportunity for someone to do an expected act or show a given response.

Greetings, in business and in personal life, play a huge role in how people respond to you. You can easily adjust and tune an expected response into something more tolerable and professional.

Example: At a truck stop recently, I witnessed a bright, cheery young lady greeting a gruff-looking trucker.

    Young lady: "Good morning, sir!"
    Trucker: "What's so damned good about it?"
    Young lady: "Hey, we're breathing and working!" she said with a smile.
    Trucker: "Yeah, I have to go do this crap again."

I'll add this now – I absolutely hate that we must tailor our greetings towards others in a manner that take their knees out and makes it where they can't bitch, whine or complain. I will say that again. I absolutely hate that we have to tailor our greetings towards others in a manner that take their knees out and makes it where they can't bitch, whine or complain. We shouldn't have to do that, but people *want* to bitch, whine, and complain, and many will jump at every opportunity to do so.

Let's change things up.

> Young lady: "Hello, sir."
> Trucker: "Hello." (upset that he can't give a speech about how bad his life is)
> Young lady: "Your coffee is $1.19. Will there be anything else?"
> Trucker: "No, thanks."
> Young lady: "Thank you, sir."

That wonderful young lady didn't have to deal with his gruff attitude and whiny story. There are several other ways to greet people or initiate conversations that can "take their knees out".

One I like is, "Hey, what's new and good?"

The person receiving your greeting can't immediately jump into complaining mode by responding to "good morning". In fact, you've challenged them to come up with something good in their life that they can tell you about.

Other greetings:

"Hey there," "Hi," "What's up?" "Sir," (said with eye contact, simple greeting), "Ma'am," (same notion). These greetings don't allow for a long response, with a laundry list of problems.

I must admit that I've gotten a bit cynical over the years, being involved with the military, the automotive industry, and the trucking/transportation/towing industries, in that I tend to respond sarcastically when a grown-up man or women choses to accost me with unsolicited whining. This is one reason I no longer ask "How are you?" "How are you doing?", "How ya' doing?", or "How's things?". Because they'll TELL you, and you may not be ready for the pathetic, extended dissertation you will be subjected to.

If I greet someone with a "what's up?", and they respond "This weather sucks and I'm tired," I'll actually stop them, make solid eye contact, and say, "Look on the bright side. It gives you something to bitch about in case you run out of things to bitch about."

Seminars

I have hosted several seminars over the years, mostly framed around employer/employee relations and intertwined with humor.

One of the first segments, while people are still filing into the room, is where I pick an older, experienced person and chat with them off-microphone. I try to pick out someone who appears to be with HR or management.

I walk up to them, engage them with a greeting, and then start bitching about everything under the sun. I start with how tired I am, how my feet hurt, I talk about my abscessed tooth, and then onto how my wife and I have been arguing…and she got so mad I had to sleep on the couch. No "action", if you know what I mean.

And I walk away, and finish prepping for the event. I watch that person circulate my story around their table to other professionals, and make note of the reaction of their table mates.

Once the event starts, back to that person is the first place I go, and I walk through our one-sided conversation and announce to the crowd everything I've said.

Imagine, if you will, if I did this to you at a seminar. Also understand that everyone judges everything they experience, and this is fair game like anything else.

How would you feel about the scenario in general?
How would you feel about me, both personally and professionally?
How would you feel about my company?
What about the value your company was getting in me as a speaker?
How would you feel about my alleged physical ailments?
What about my ability to take care of myself, physically and medically?
Would you wonder why the heck I was telling you all of this?
What if I found out that you told everyone at your table about me?

Let's go over each one and drop in some of our personal thoughts. I'll add mine, as if someone had approached me in this way, and you work on yours.

How would you feel about the scenario in general?

I would feel a little disgusted by the guy. I mean, he's here to help train our people, and he's dropping all this whiny personal crap on me. Why me?

How would you feel about me, both personally and professionally?

I think the guy is a schmuck. He can't handle his own life, so why is he here trying to tell us how to handle ours? And he gets paid for this?

How would you feel about my company?

People talk, plus the guy probably needs references. If he gets a bunch of bad reviews, he won't be in business long.

What about the value your company was getting in me as a speaker?

Where did the CEO come up with this guy? Was he doing stand-up at the Waffle House? I hope they're not paying him more than twenty bucks, and I hope there's donuts in the back of the room.

How would you feel about my alleged physical ailments?

Seems like the guy should get some good exercise, maybe buy better shoes, get more rest, whatever. What a whiner.

What about my ability to take care of myself, physically and medically?

If the guy can't take care of himself, he probably can't take care of his house or his wife. No wonder he had to sleep on the couch.

Would you wonder why the heck I was telling you all of this?

Right. Why me? I don't want to hear all of this personal crap. Don't you have some speaker stuff to do?

What if I found out that you told everyone at your table about me?

You dropped all this stuff on me without regard for anyone hearing it – I just passed on what I was told.

Why aren't you working?

I didn't see you coming.

There's no narrative here, just something to think on. Think about that one for a while, and how it applies to your situation.

Smoke/Coffee/Water Breaks

No, I'm not implying you should run your office or warehouse like the old ships where the guys were below deck rowing and getting beaten with whips. People are entitled to breaks by state and federal law, and you should never compromise your business by cutting into these required breaks.

I am, however, guaranteeing you that breaks are being abused. It's a fact, and in most workplaces. It's also disguised as an attempt at working, but on its face, it's a break, and it's likely much longer than you think.

While studying sociology during active duty, this very topic of how people stretch the limits of the rules and their employer's patience into more personal time at work. My sociology professor tasked us to pay attention to certain behaviors, and account for the time spent. My primary target was smoke breaks. In a commander's staff situation where a group of people work in an office environment, smoking may be a main distraction. It certainly was during my survey.

Smoke breaks generally go far beyond company policies and state laws on employee breaks, and turn into social occasions. Two of the men in my office were smokers, and two were not, myself included. We were allowed to breaks as needed, and I'd go to the restroom or get a soda, taking around fifteen minutes per half day for break time. Thirty minutes per day, not counting lunch. That's two and a half hours in a week. That's also the standard in many companies for breaks.

I started noting the time the other guys would take for smoke breaks. Our building had a back porch, and several people would gravitate out there, especially first thing in the morning, right after lunch, and about thirty minutes before quitting time.

Of the two smokers, one man was worse than the other, and regularly spent three and a half hours per day on the "smoking porch." The other man averaged just over two hours. In my experience since then, in a variety of shops, offices, warehouses, and stores, these numbers are still very common.

Three and a half hours per day. Heck, let's look at the lesser offender. Two hours and ten minutes per day, averaged over a week. That's ten hours and fifty minutes per week. Let's look at the difference between that guy and me. Eight hours and twenty minutes.

At $18.00 an hour, that's actually $25.20 when you multiply it by 1.4. $25.20 x 8.33 hours is $209.92 per week, or $10,915.84.00 per year. And that's on the light side. Many smokers are more like the first guy at 3.5 hours per day – and that's $441.00 per week and $22,932.00 out of your company's pocket.

Revenue is revenue. What you do with your policies and enforcement is up to you.

Social Media

Facebook, Instagram, Twitter, and even supposedly professional LinkedIn allows for a constant barrage of whining. From a business perspective, if you have a company Facebook page, for example, a written policy should be in place to curtail employees from posting negative things, even seemingly harmless items like "working overtime again ☹".

Managers and business owners who "friend" their employees are asking for a double-whammy when it comes to complaining, bitching, and whining…and gossip.

Common Facebook whines are "I'm tired," "I hate working night shift," or "Judy in accounting is a b****." Facebook, like MySpace before it, gives the whiner or complainer a speaking platform to write all the negative things they like.

My suggestion is to avoid being linked with your employees, and post only professional items on your company Facebook page. Having a central person as the primary admin on the page, and having all posts by others require approval allows the admin person to cull the whiny or other unprofessional posts from the herd.

7-11 Guy

A little background. It was 2003, and my oldest son had been diagnosed in early 2002 with Large Cell Non-Hodgkin's Lymphoma, Stage 2, and given ninety days to live. We'd gotten past the ninety days, thankfully, and my wife took a leave of absence from her job, we were making daily trips from Lansdale, PA into Philadelphia just about every day that he wasn't doing an inpatient treatment.

I was working at a lawfirm doing expert witness work and had a good insurance plan, but Blue Cross had just let us know that we'd hit the $1 million lifetime cap and they weren't paying past the first of the next month.

My wife was exhausted, as she slept on a cot next to my son's bed. I'd go downtown every night when he was in the cancer ward and talk with her and eat a meal. We were wiped out.

On the job front, the gig was going pretty well, and since I was testifying in court three or four days per week, and I'd started the job with only two nice suits, I started buying a suit every other week or so. These weren't high-dollar, and I usually got the from K&G Men's Store or Burlington Coat Factory. I had a strong complement of dress shirts, ties, and shoes, and usually got plenty of compliments, even though I had a fairly cheap wardrobe. This particular day, I was wearing a dark olive double-breasted suit

($89), brown Stacy Adams ($39) shoes, a pale yellow shirt ($12) and brown and gold print tie ($7).

I told you all of that to tell you this.

We had one car, a nice older Mustang GT, and that day it was with my wife at the hospital. One of the attorneys I worked with dropped me off at the hospital this one day so I could drive my son and wife home, as he'd just finished a treatment. My son's doctor begged him to eat, but he didn't want much, since the medication left him with a metallic taste in his mouth and nothing tasted good to him.
On this day, I bugged him all the way back to our town about what he wanted to eat. He finally gave in and requested Twinkies and a Mountain Dew. Done. I didn't have a lot of money until payday since we were spending money hand over foot with our travels, but inside the 7-11 in Ambler, PA I charged.

I went to the cooler and grabbed him a Mountain Dew, and got a Diet Coke for me and a water for my wife. I then picked up a pack of Twinkies and walked to the counter. There was an older woman in front of me, just finishing her transaction and putting things back in her purse. As I fell into line behind her, and older man and younger woman got in line behind me.

As the lady moved aside, I set my things down and took in the appearance of the man behind the counter. He was around forty, hadn't shaved in a week, needed a haircut, his issued 7-11 shirt was dirty as if he'd worn it for a week, and it had had fresh stains down the front. His shirt was partially untucked, and his nametag was crooked.

I greeted him with "Hey, how ya' doing?"

And he replied with a gnarly attitude, "What the f*** do you care in your thousand-dollar suit?"

(Please bear in mind this area had many legal and medical firms nearby, so many people were in and out of the store in high-end clothing)

I looked out to my old Mustang, seeing my wife asleep in the front seat and my son with a blank stare on his face. I looked at the lady to my side, still arranging her purse, and glanced back to the man and woman behind me, searching their faces to see if they'd heard what he said. Their shocked looks told me they had.

I asked the two women and the man if they minded if I responded to him.

"No, you go right ahead," was the general consensus.

"Dude," I began. "Look out there at that 1986 Mustang GT. It's my only car, and it has 176,000 miles on it. See that kid in the back seat that looks like Casper the Ghost? He has no pigment left in his skin and no hair on his body because he's got cancer and his going through chemotherapy and radiation. The lady in the front seat is my wife. She had to quit her job to take care of him when he's in the hospital. He just finished a ten-day treatment."

The man muttered something, but I continued.

"This isn't a thousand-dollar suit. This is an eighty-nine-dollar suit. Hell, the whole set of clothes I have on doesn't break a hundred and fifty. I look good because I take care of my body and know how to match and wear my clothes."

I was just warming up and going into drill sergeant mode as my tone raised substantially, and his manager came out of her office.

"Let's talk about you for a moment. It seems you're not happy with your station in life, so you need to talk trash to someone who is. I asked you how you were because I genuinely care about people, and you're part of that group, do you understand?"

He nodded.

"If you're not happy with where you are or what you're doing, do take it out on me or anyone else. You're wearing dirty clothes, your hygiene sucks, and you evidently hate you job. Those things are easy to fix. Get a different job. Clean yourself up. Ask for a promotion. Go back to school. Whatever it takes. Am I clear?"

"Yes," he nodded.

"Good, because I come in here several times a week because you sell canned Diet Cokes for sixty-nine cents, and I'll be back soon. When I come in, I'm going to ask you again how you're doing, and if you don't respond with fine a damned dandy, I'm going to take you outside and sweep the parking lot with you, using your ass as a broom!"

I paid and left, and my wife asked me what all of that was about. "Nothing to worry about, babe," I responded.

I didn't go over this personal story to accomplish anything except to show you how some people act when given the chance to complain. This guy didn't even start with basic annoying, unprofessional whining, he got belligerent and challenged a regular customer who was being friendly to the clerk and everyone else in the store.

As a manager, the store manager failed by allowing a guy with a bad attitude, and bad appearance and hygiene to work a very visible position. A manager's complacent, unobserving attitude can lead to bad news for your business.

Most people, when spoken to any unprofessional manner, would simply find another store to frequent as you watch your sales numbers drop like an anvil on Jupiter.

Station in life

I like to use the phrase "station in life" because it is an active notion that describes your current situation or the one you want to be in or are working towards.

The guy in the 7-11 story didn't like his station in life and he was miserable. And it showed. It showed in his appearance, his hygiene, and his attitude. He hated his job, and he was going to make sure everyone knew it, hopefully so they'd feel sorry for him. To what end, I don't know.

You may be working at a fast food restaurant while going to night school, and even though you're not working your dream job just yet, that is your current station in life.

OWN IT. Don't be ashamed of it, and don't complain about it. That is, if you know it's a temporary fit and you're just passing through. You might be surprised how many future chances and connections can be generated while you're doing a job that is less than desirable or pays less than you'd like.

If you're a coffee mixologist or a fry cook at a burger joint, be professional. That old guy in the suit and tie owns a lawfirm, and since you're in law school, the LAST thing you'd want to do is complain about your job or bitch about life.

Greet them, get to know them, and try to cultivate a connection. Even if they're not hiring, they likely know someone who is. Strike up a conversation with a smile on your face, have a clean outfit on, and make sure they know what you're doing outside of work and where you're trying to go.

I can't imagine how many missed opportunities there are when someone is working what they perceive as a dead-end job, and they're standing around whining about work. Your customers HEAR you. They can read your face, and read your attitude.

I've hired several sales interns and full-time employees out of customer service or fast food positions simply because I liked their attitude and smile. I found out they were working on a degree, and it was aligned with what I was doing. If they had a bad attitude or weren't professional and engaging, I would have never encountered them and given them the opportunity.

OWN your job, even if it's low-paying and you're just passing through. You never know what impact that temporary job may have on your career - connections gained.

Now, with that said, ask yourself how many times you've walked into a convenience store, restaurant, bar, or other retail establishment and the person you contacted appeared to watch the clock like a hawk, and they were in the starting blocks for the race out the door.

Were they like my sandwich shop guy? Or the 7-11 guy?

Are these people you might want to hire, or do you look past them like they're not there?

Even if you, as a manager, are in somewhat of a temporary position, OWN it, and be the best you can be. Your professionalism will shine above that of other people and you will be recognized. Fact of life. If you don't show up with a smile and great outlook, though, I can guarantee that the only thing you'll be noticed for is a sour attitude. No opportunities for you!

Lynn and the flat tire

I worked at a large lawfirm near Philadelphia for several years, as I mentioned in the 7-11 guy story. When my son was diagnosed with cancer, the managing partner agreed to let me come and go as I needed to visit my son. I worked from home, writing reports, fielding phone calls and emails, and would go to court whenever necessary. We lived only a block from the firm, and I'd walk there, carrying a box of files, drop them off with the respective attorney or clerk, and pick up new files for expert reports.

The day before the incident I'll explain, Lynn had a flat tire on her car while on her way to work. She was two hours late, had to wait for AAA to change the tire, and then was faced with having to take the tire to Pep Boys to get the flat repaired and the original tire and wheel reinstalled on her car.

I happened to be in the firm when she arrived that day, and was totally distraught, on the verge of tears, and appeared to act like a normal person would if they'd almost been hit by a bus or were a victim of an armed robbery. Several of the other legal clerks comforted and consoled her after her harrowing ordeal. I rolled my eyes and continued about my day.

The next day, while dropping off and picking up files, I entered the building with my usual smile and greetings, saying hello to everyone as I walked through. Lynn stopped me, and actually took my hand. She got very quiet and serious.

Lynn: "Jay, you're remarkable."
Me: "Why do you say that?"
Lynn: "You come in and out every day, and always have a smile on your face and talk to people, and your son is going through cancer treatment. How do you do it?"
Me: "Do what?"
Lynn: "Keep a smile on your face when such bad things are going on."
Me: "Lynn, look. I've cried a couple of times. I get worried. I also know that I'm that boy's dad, and he needs me to go to work, do the best job I can do, and keep a good attitude. The last thing he needs is me in the fetal position on the floor, crying like a baby, yelling about giving up or whatever."
Lynn: "Well, it's remarkable."
Me: "Can I give you some advice?"
She nodded.

"Look, you had a flat tire, and maybe that was your first one, but it's just a damned tire. Your car didn't catch on fire. You didn't have a wreck. Your kid didn't get hit by the school bus. A TIRE. It cost you $20 to get fixed, and AAA even came out and changed it for you. Worst case scenario, you'd have to replace the tire and you're out a hundred bucks.

Here's something to think about. If you get that damned worked up over a damned tire, what are you going to do when you have a real problem? Put on your big girl panties, handle the problem, and press on. I promise you, if a flat tire freaks you out, you're going to be of ZERO VALUE to your child if they break an arm on the playground.

Do yourself a favor. Lose the drama, reevaluate everything, and then decide the things that you really should get upset about. A tire isn't one of them."

Walmart tire guys

I know that Walmart is an easy target for picking on, but this scenario was just dumb.

Three weeks ago, I bought new tires for my Chevrolet Silverado, had ordered them through Walmart, and my wife had them mounted and balanced while I was out of town. We had to make an emergency trip to Pennsylvania the next week, and noticed a vibration at highway speeds. Nice tires, since I don't buy junk, and a fairly new truck...I shouldn't have a vibration.

I brought the truck back after returning from our trip, and learned way more than I should have about the tire department at my local Walmart.

When I first entered, I was told by a tire technician that I'd need an invoice. Behind the counter was a guy with a manager nametag on, and I asked if he would print out my invoice. He said he didn't know how. Really? Give me that name tag!!
There was a lady behind him, and he turned to her, as I did, and she shrugged her shoulders and walked into an office.

One other clerk was there, an older guy – I asked if he would print the invoice, and he started whining about it being Monday and having to look up my name and my truck, scoffing and exhaling loudly the whole time. Imagine a pouting seven-year-old asking, "Okay, what's your name?" as they were just put on restriction.

After being in the waiting room an hour or so, "Marvin", a thirty-ish black guy, approached me and began explaining the reason why they couldn't balance my tires. He had been the person who wrote up the repair order.

Marvin explained that the young guy who was working on my truck had no idea what he was doing. He explained that he didn't know how to set up the balancer, either. This other young guy was wasting the stick-on balancing weights, and in fact, had exhausted their supply of the weights after only two of my tires.

I countered respectfully that I understood that Marvin didn't know how to use the equipment, and that the other guy didn't, either. I asked if anyone there could successfully set up the balancer (program it for my wheel style, diameter, and width), and Marvin replied that yes, the old guy out there could do it just fine. The problem was that the old guy was a jerk, and that he wouldn't train either of the younger men, and wouldn't work on my truck since the one guy had already started working.

So….I'm just wanting my tires balanced better, and because an old gruff guy can't get along with his coworkers and won't help train them, I lose? Nothing gets done?

The one young guy did do some balancing work, and when I drove the truck home, it was a hundred times worse than before.

I called and talked to a manager, since I'd be out of town again when my wife could take the truck in again, and wanted to him to make sure they had an adequate supply of stick-on weights and someone versed on the machine...so we could get the truck handled correctly. The manager said he'd "Try", and would leave a note for the other manager. Sheesh.

Think about this for a moment. I contacted six people at this Walmart. Only one, Marvin, was positive. Everyone else had an attitude problem, or simply didn't want to do their job. They'll likely have a pow-wow on company time later and complain about how hard their job is and how tough it is to deal with jerks like me (I wasn't).

Why did I, as a customer, need to know about the lack of training, incompetence, and especially the unprofessional attitude issues between the three guys in the shop?

How much easier would their respective jobs have been if they would have just smiled and did their tasks? I just can't imagine going through life shirking responsibility and being miserable, and those situations aren't exclusive to Walmart or any other store chain.

Cancer ward nurse

Another event from the time my son was in treatment comes to mind, and will hopefully show you just how ignorant complainers are of other people's issues and priorities.

We were completely thankful for all the nurses on staff, both in the cancer ward and the clinic. The cancer ward was a small facility on the top floor of the hospital, and had eight rooms with single twin hospital beds, a television, and each room had its own bathroom with a shower. As the year and a half that my son was in treatment progressed, we got to know many of the other children in treatment, along with their parents.

We parents would "spell" other parents so they could go to the cafeteria and eat, grab a shower, or go home for a while, and we'd play games with the kids, or just sit and talk. I got to know some really cool kids, going through the same rough time as my son, and unfortunately, we lost several children along the way.

One of the most precious kids was seven-year-old redhaired girl who'd been diagnosed with leukemia at age six. She had also lost both her legs at age three when her brother had just gotten his license, was in a hurry to leave the house, and back over here while she was riding her tricycle in the driveway.

Even with no legs and a bad diagnosis, she was upbeat, smiling, and played a mean game of Uno.

One of the nurses was a forty-ish lady who sauntered around the ward in a lazy fashion. She was always complaining about being tired, or having to work in place of someone else, or having to work twelve-hour shifts. Think for a moment what all the kids are parents were dealing with in this ward…

On this particular day, my son had a bad incident with his meds, and was throwing up violently. We were trying to keep him calm, and he'd been in for seven days, and was at the end of his rope. He was tired of it all, was crying, and in pain. He'd been dealing with this for too long.

The little redhead wasn't her spritely self that day, either, although since I'd just arrived, I hadn't talked to her.

I left to go downstairs and get my wife some coffee, and I quickly walked past the nurses' station and greeted the three paddies working there. The sauntering nurse was on the far end. I must apologize in advance because I lost my mind after I greeted her and got her response.

"Miss Diana, how you doing?"
"Oh, Mister Lewis, I'm *tired* (drawn out) and my feet hurt."

I lost it.

"Diana, I want you to look in that room right there with that pretty little girl with red hair. You see her?!" I shouted.

She was taken aback by my raised voice, but nodded.

"She wishes she had feet to hurt! She doesn't have any feet! She doesn't have any legs! She lost them, and is sick, and is only seven! She wished she had feet to hurt and wasn't sick! If so, she's be out running and riding bikes with the other kids in her neighborhood and laughing and hollering."

I calmed somewhat and spoke quieter.

"She wishes she had feet to hurt, and you're up here making a buttload of money, doing a job where you sit all day, and then you WALK outside and go home to your family, and you're in good health! And you want to sit around and bitch about things that these kids WISH they could experience? Shame on you, woman. Shame on you."

I walked out and immediately wished I hadn't lost my temper, as I made Diana cry. I know the little girl heard me, too, but doggone it, she'd heard Diana's whining as well. I went downstairs and returned without making eye contact.

Because of that incident, I started using a sentence – "Be careful who you complain to." And it's true, you never know what that other person is going through. They may have lost a child, been served with divorce papers, had their only car blow up, and you're over here complaining about something totally trivial.

Love's in West Memphis, Arkansas

During an emergency road trip, I rolled through Arkansas and into Tennessee, stopping in West Memphis to get fuel and some drinks.

I went inside in a hurry and grabbed a bottle of water for my wife and a soda for me, and hurried to the counter. There were two young ladies behind the counter, and they made eye contact as I walked up. I smiled and greeted both of them, and they turned towards each other as one lady showed the other lady something on her Facebook page. I was a little shocked that after they both made eye contact with me, they completely disregarded their duties and had better things to do.

I looked down at the counter. It was a mess, as someone had spilled soda all over, and there were several sticky circles from soda cans covering the counter. Behind the counter, trash was on the floor, along with dirt and debris. I looked out toward my truck. The glass on the doors was filthy, as was the glass on the large fixed windows adjacent to the doors. The floor of the store was nasty and stained, and likely had not been mopped with good cleaner in over a week.

As I turned my eyes back to the ladies, they broke up their Facebook session and with attitude, asked if I needed anything else.

I shrugged and paid, shaking my head. I thought of all the things wrong with the place, and wondered what the manager was doing. I also made a pledge to never go there again.

Bob's Janitorial Supply

I was in a janitorial supply business in Mississippi a while back. I witnessed employee apathy where I can't exactly place a value on the lost revenue.

I was in the lobby and a young man, who appeared to be a manager or clerk, was talking to a buddy about their recent hunting trip. The phone was ringing like crazy. I looked at the business phone, and all four lines were going. He and his buddy had been talking for over fifteen minutes. I was waiting for the owner, who would arrive a little later. Meanwhile, Jethro and Bubba were discussing white tail deer.

Even "Bubba" (the name I assigned to his buddy) asked the employee, "Aren't you going to answer that?"

His reply was "They'll call back."

Bear in mind that another young man had taken a phone order right after I arrived, but then went into the warehouse to do some work. The person calling in had ordered several items that the young man repeated back – two cases of paper towels, two eight-packs of toilet paper, two gallons of bleach, and a gallon of degreaser.

This was a fairly small town, and likely the only janitorial supply business in town.

Ask yourself, please, the same questions I asked myself:

With four lines ringing, and some calls falling off, how many calls do you think the guy missed in fifteen minutes?

How often does this happen?

When would you call for janitorial supplies, in order to "get your order in"? I'd call first thing in the morning. Would you?

(The boss/owner doesn't come in until the business has been open for an hour, by the way.)

If you assigned an average dollar amount to an order, what would it be? Gross profit on each order? Multiplied by how many lost orders?

How long would you let the phone ring before you sent one of your employees down to the big box store to pick up cleaning supplies?

Do the math. What do you think this owner is losing by not being in the store when it opens, and how much as "Jethro" cost the owner in lost sales?

Gossip

In the workplace, I believe all forms of gossip should be prohibited, addressed early and strongly as gossip is a cancer that eats at the core of an organization. You cannot do your best as a member of any team if you harbor ill feelings towards, or worse yet, believe untrue stories about your team members.

Gossip is a form of distraction that can lead to apathy about the job since it can be viewed as entertaining. Many people thoroughly enjoy hearing all the scoop on someone else, especially if it is particularly juicy, involves some public meltdown, laws broken, or relationship drama.

By its very nature, gossip turns a quick meeting to line out people for a task into a two-hour session akin The Young And The Restless. People are naturally drawn into gossip, just like when you pass an accident on the road, people feel compelled to slow down and gawk for the details. It also happens when you pass someone who has been pulled over by the police – people want to see if they're having their vehicle searched, or if it's someone they know.

Gossip can also be work-related. It can involve discussing wages, benefits, seniority, promotions, special projects, and other things.

I did several surveys before starting this book. In my experience, I had several part-time jobs in high school and then went into the military. In the military, everyone can easily figure out how much another person is paid by knowing their rank and their time in service. Because this subject is open and obvious, it isn't an issue in the military.

In the civilian world, though, three people doing the same job could make a largely different amount of money per hour or as a salary.

My first hourly job after entering the military was a part-time gig at a home improvement center as a truck driver. It was 1987 and I was twenty-three. I was hired in at $9.91 an hour, mainly because the boss assumed I'd be reliable, and I had a Class A commercial driver's license. The first evening I worked, the whole group of us drivers and yard works jumped in to straighten up the yard for a visiting vice president. I jumped in and starting working with three of the yard guys, introduced myself and starting helping out. One of the guys asked what my job was and how much I made. I explained that I was a delivery driver, and I made $9.91 an hour. The young man was angry and stated that he only made $6.50 an hour, and he'd been there for a year. Minimum wage at the time was $6.25.

Within thirty minutes, I was called into the manager's office, briefed on my mistake, and told that if I ever discussed wages again, I'd be fired on the spot.

My surveys showed that at least 95% of the people surveyed had the same opinion from their current and previous jobs.

I can certainly imagine that I'd be upset if a new guy made more than I did, especially if I'd been on the job for quite a while. Also, things like race, sex, ethnicity, and personal relations come into play, and people with a chip on their shoulder are just looking for an opportunity to bitch, moan, and whine…and finding out that the new black guy makes more than they do could lead to an eruption of volcanic proportions. Same with male versus female.

My recommendation is to have a strong and unwavering policy where all employees must avoid any discussions involving wages, overtime, benefits, seniority, or special projects. To allow wide open discussions is to guarantee some hard feelings. If an employee doesn't make a big deal of it on the surface, it can produce resentment and be a great motivation for looking for a new job. A good way to lose good employees.

Also on the gossip subject is the actual time involved and what it costs you.

Per the Bureau of Labor and Statistics, the national average for the factor of employee cost is 1.4. For this example, I'm going to use $15.00 per hour and 40 hours per week. My point here is that for every wasted hour in a week, you're not just out the $15.00, you're out that amount multiplied by 1.4, since you match things like Social Security, Unemployment, Medicare, and state/local/ federal taxes. That's $21.00 an hour per person. If two employees gossip for only two hours per week, that's $21.00 x 2 x 2, or $84.00 per week. It's super easy to tally two hours of gossiping when you get five minutes here and ten minutes there. $84.00 for those two employees turns into $336.00 per month or…get this…$4,368.00 per year. Off your bottom line.

What could you do with an extra $4,368 in productivity and revenue? How many people in the work area of those two employees stop what they're doing to listen in?

Specific gossip or self-revelation areas to avoid:

Follow the example of the medical community. The Health Insurance Portability and Accountability Act, or HIIPA is designed to protect the privacy standards to protect patient's medical records and information. This includes information provided to health plans, doctors, nurses, and other health car providers. Essentially, it is forbidden to discuss a patient's medical information in any public area or where other people may hear.

I dropped in that long-winded, but necessary explanation to emphasize the notion that NO ONE wants to know about your hemorrhoids, erectile dysfunction, or recent surgery.

Let's harken back to the days where people simply didn't discuss these significantly personal topics, and a woman's issues with her menstrual cycle was referred to as "female problems." With that said, "a medical issue", as explanation for someone's absence is all the definition you need. After all, telling more is gossip that will spread like wildfire.

Another area to avoid discussing at work is details of a relationship or most especially, your sex life. Quite simply, this is work, and your conquests from the club last night have nothing to do with the tasks you're assigned to do. As we all can testify, I'm sure, I'm had some incredibly personal information volunteered to me over the years. I really didn't want to know that the middle-aged guy and his wife were into swapping with other couples, and no, I didn't need details.

In 1987, I was stationed in Abilene, Texas, and worked part-time delivering pizza for Scooter's Pizza. Great pizza, but the business died.

In one discussion that has haunted me now for thirty years was where I was in the shop, along with a cook, a manager, and an assistant manager. The assistant manager was tall, but heavy, and his personal appearance was always funky. Always needed to shave, clothes were dirty, he smelled musty, etc. He would show us all photos of when he was in high school and college, and he was slim and trim, and a decent-looking guy.

This one night he was giving our cook a hard time because it was common knowledge that the cook's new girlfriend kept him "tired." Dan, the musty-smelling guy, stated that he wished he was getting laid more often.

The cook asked what happened. Did his wife get fat and mean or something?

Dan replied that, "No, she didn't get fat. I did. I've gained eighty pounds in the two years since we got married. She's also taking this antihistamine for her allergies, and it makes her vagina dry."

Really, Dan??

People also freely discuss legal issues, jail time, jail time for relatives…."Dang, I was up late last night, had to bail the brother-in-law out of jail again for beating my sister…"

You may have a good opinion of someone, only to find out they're a felon. Or they pass that information on about another employee.

And that nugget of information wasn't listed on their employment application. See where this goes?

People talk about potential lawsuits, child custody, divorce, real estate, or inheritance issues, and it is all time occupying, costly to you, and unprofessional.

Complaining as a Dialect or Language

Actual discussion heard recently in a truck stop in Benton, Arkansas:

"Why were you late this morning?" the manager asked.
"I had to let my car warm up for like twenty minutes, and then there was frost, and the defrost thing wouldn't make it go away, and I had to use one of them ice pick things to scrape the window," the young man explained.
"You didn't know it was going to dip below freezing? It's the middle of November," the boss added. The young man gave a blank look.
"Well, we needed you hear at six. It was almost 6:30 when you clocked in," the manager stated.
"I know, yeah, I'll try to do better," the young man offered.

I had to shake my head. Everyone has a phone, especially young people. Everyone has an Android or iPhone, and all you have to do to check the weather is hit a quick app, or like on my phone, touch the location and temperature icon and it gives you weather for that day and the next few days.

I'd have to have a significant chat with this young man about personal responsibility. That is mainly because after the boss talked to him, he walked directly over to the cashier and started going off about what a jerk the boss was, how he chewed him out for being late, and that it wasn't his fault that there was frost on his car. I gathered my items and left, and the young guy's mouth was still running, and I predicted his diatribe would continue for quite a while.

Many people won't take responsibility for their actions, or do preventive measures like checking the weather or allowing for things like Daylight Savings Time. It's always someone else's fault. Because of this, most of them have developed complaining as an actual language or dialect. They can't communicate unless they're whining.

Guy walks in at work.
"Man, I had to work two extra hours of overtime last night. I didn't get home until 8. Rhonda was all kinds of pissed."

Second guy can't leave this alone.

"At least you get overtime. You must have your nose up the boss's ass. I haven't had any overtime for months. And I'm only making $10.00 an hour. This job sucks."

First guy: "I'm not kissing the boss's ass. I just work harder than you. You're the one always calling out of work. That's why I get the overtime. I get $12.00 an hour, though. If you weren't a little bitch, you'd get a raise, too. I just hate working extra. It always happens when somebody calls out. I wish it was more predictable."

Second guy: "How can it be predictable when somebody calls out? You bitch too much. Man, $12.00 an hour? And I've been here longer than you?"

First guy: "I don't bitch near as much as Roger. That guy is always whining."

Two truckers heard recently:

First guy: "This job sucks. I hate driving so much and trying to deal with traffic."

Second guy (a competitor): "I know what you mean. My dispatcher always sends me on loads through Atlanta, and Atlanta's traffic sucks."

First guy: "Yeah, I go through there about once a week."

Second guy: "Once a week? I'm through there at least *three* times a week, sometimes *four or five*. Once a week ain't shit."

First guy (turns into a competitor or one-up): "Oh yeah? One time last month I was through Atlanta twice a day for a week. Twelve times through Atlanta!"

My point to all of this is that these guys were on the clock d getting ready to make deliveries. If this is a daily "bitch session", they could easily hit two or three hours of whining per week. With a driver making $18.00 an hour, times two for two drivers, plus the 1.4 factor that it actually costs you as an employer, that's $25.20 per hour, per person.

Two people standing there for fifteen minutes per day equals one-hundred-fifty minutes of clock time. 2.5 hours. That's $63.00 a week for a quick bitching session each day. $3,276.00 a year in lost production.

Physical Impact of Negative Behavior

Author LC Hawkley wrote in the book "Brain, Behavior, and Immunity" that a five- to ten-minute episode of negative behavior, examples given are being angry, active complaining, allowing yourself to be very frustrated (without due cause, as it makes a difference) can have a four- to five-hour significant impact on your body's immune system. Your body's ability to ward off illness is reduced by the changed chemical balance in your body as brought on by these emotions. Combine a few tantrums or whining sessions with the time stamp of the cold and flu season, and you may end up with a significant winter illness. If you perpetuate this illness by continuing to be negative, like whining because you're sick, you'll likely *extend* and *increase* the duration and severity of the illness.

On the other side of that, having a positive experience, like someone thanking you (sincerely) for help on the job, a compliment by a coworker, or a happy phone call from your spouse or significant other can *improve* your immune system for up to twenty-four hours. This is because all of these positive experiences produce endorphins. This fact is why I always recommend that you handle stressful family business at home, since getting into a shouting match with your husband or wife drops you into the previous category. Have employees plan ahead, and try to work out friendly, supportive phone calls or notes from home. There's nothing like having an argument with your spouse, even over something trivial, while you're at work and you can't leave. It will occupy your mind for the rest of the day. It's only natural. That's also when you "vent" to your buddy at the water cooler about your "nagging wife" ...and a five-minute break turns into a forty-five-minute complaint session.

$20.00 an hour, per person, is a true cost of $28.00. Times two is $56.00. At forty-five minutes, that three-minute argument with his wife and resulting whine session with his coworker cost you, as an employer, $42.00.

If you factor in the mental aspect of this spousal argument, my guess is that it would take the husband or wife at least two hours to get back into the game. That's another $56.00. Then, you'll have the follow-up session tomorrow when the coworker asks the husband is the wife is still mad. There's another hour, and then another hour for the guy to get back on task and focus. Counting the two employees down for an hour the next day and the hour to refocus, that's an additional $84.00.

Most people who put their business "in the street" or "air dirty laundry" at work don't limit these incidents to one a year. It's usually a regular occurrence, and likely weekly or monthly at least. This again reflects on the level of professionalism they have and the measure of control you have.

At $42.00, plus $56.00, plus $84.00, per week, that's $184.00 per week and $9,464.00 in a year. Can you afford $9,464 in lost revenue or productivity?

Can you stop an employee from having an argument with his wife on company time? Yes and no. Depends on how long and how thoroughly your indoctrination briefing is. I'll address these initial briefings, as well as limiting the gossip affect after a personal issue in the next few chapters.

My research shows that in normal conversations, people complain once per minute. I realize this is a generalization, but I challenge you to sit back and listen to a conversation, perhaps on a bus, in another public place, or even during a family gathering. People love to complain. It feels good, and beckons sympathy. The problem is that it becomes a learned behavior – we rewire our brains to complain and look at the negative side of things. And that causes physical and mental health issues.

The Mood-Dependent Workplace

It's easy to tell of you have a mood-dependent workplace. Is there a man or woman who exudes their mood on their sleeve, and people purposely avoid them when they're in a bad mood, or work to be extra productive when they're in a good mood?

I worked at a nationally-accredited technical training school, and shortly after starting there, was warned by many of the students to avoid "Natalie", the school director's secretary, during certain times of the week or month. Evidently, Natalie would argue with her husband, or have a physical or medical condition, and would aggressively take it out on students and staff members.

A little background. This school was huge, with almost 2,000 students. Instructors and education managers would usually staff the halls and entrances to greet students, establish relationships, and correct dress code violations. For example, a student had to wear an approved school shirt and have their student ID badge hanging from their lanyard. If these two elements weren't present, they were sent home. Same with work boots. No sneakers allowed.

We instructors would firmly but politely make these corrections, but Natalie would rip into students like a drill sergeant. I made the mistake of talking to her after she'd screamed at one of my sons (a student there). Big mistake, evidently, as she started the ball rolling to try to get me fired. I was blown away, as I'd never seen anything like it.

She had the "Queen Bee" syndrome going, and if her mood wasn't cheery, you'd better run.

I lost count of the time spent in class trying to talk students out of quitting and transferring to another school. These students worked hard, usually didn't have much money, maintained part-time jobs and were paying close to twenty grand for the year.

The least thing any of them needed was a power-tripping admin person taking out her personal moodiness on innocent people.

Perhaps you have a "Natalie" on your staff. If you aren't stopping their actions with a very firm hand, you're enabling them, and likely alienating your entire staff. People like Natalie are very insecure and need to control everything around them. They're also very fragile, but they'd never let you see it. They cover their insecurities by demanding that others alter their actions to suit the "Queen Bee." When challenged, they become mean and vindictive, as immaturity is usually the driving force, and they simply can't act like an adult and resolve an issue. Name-calling, yelling, screaming, etc., may result. They'll swear they'll quit and they'll sue you. Do yourself a favor – have a witness of the same sex with you when you confront them. It will save you trouble later. And terminate or reassign. I don't usually promote blanket termination, but with this type of person, you'll likely have no choice. And your staff will thank you daily.

It's not always a "Queen Bee" – could be a man. The same behavior and causes are in place. If you don't get a firm hold on their actions and stop them, they'll essentially run your business into the ground for you.

Shopping Mall Security Guard Stereotype

I'm really not trying to pick on shopping mall security guards, but you must admit there's a stereotype that entails a guy or girl who wanted to be a police officer or enter the military and for some reason, couldn't. They then walk around the mall – in some cases with a drill sergeant- or state trooper-style campaign (Smokey Bear) hat, enforcing the rules against kids running, and promising to call someone with real authority if there is an actual crime.

Where I'm going with this is that we often see this stereotypical aggressive authoritarian person in many positions in retail and factory work. The customer service person who authorizes returns. The security guard at the shipper or receiver where a trucker goes to pick up or drop off freight. Even the young man taking tickets at the movie theater who gets all kinds of bent out of shape if you tear your movie tickets for him – that's HIS job.

These authoritarian personality types are a severe detriment to your business. They continually make people angry, feel inadequate, or just out of place, and more importantly drive customers and employees away from your business. Much like the Queen or King Bee mentioned in the last chapter, or the mood-driven workplace, these people need to be identified and counseled. It might be better to move them to a position where authority isn't theirs to wield.

There's an old saying, and it applies equally to men and women:

If you want to see a man's true character, give him authority.

Sometimes, you may not like what you see.

Please understand that anyone fitting the Queen or King Bee segment, or those whose mood dictates the pleasure or displeasure in operation of their whole section, are BULLIES.

A bully may project his or her own feelings of vulnerability onto the target(s) of the bullying activity. Despite the fact that a bully's typically denigrating activities are aimed at the bully's targets, the true source of such negativity is ultimately almost always found in the bully's own sense of personal insecurity and/or vulnerability.

I'll address this in solutions.

Other areas to avoid

Politics – we've seen in the recent Presidential election just how heated things can get. I can't count the number of times I've had someone make a blanket statement to me about "voting them all out" or something similar. It is my personal policy that I do not discuss politics in public with anyone. I have a very small circle when it comes to these discussions – my mother-in-law, my good friend Chris, whom I've known thirty-three years, and…yep, that's it. If you open yourself up to a political discussion, you run at least a fifty percent chance of making someone mad. Anger leads to resentment and grudges, and these lead to gossip, and you have a pissed off staff wasting time trashing each other's political views instead of working.

Religion – Just like politics, religion is a very personal subject that many people can become incensed over. In any group of six or seven people, you could easily have a Protestant Christian, a Jew, a Catholic, a Jehovah's Witness, an Atheist, an Agnostic, and a Muslim.

Again, while I'm not politically correct, I won't go out of my way to annoy or anger someone. Wishing a Muslim "Merry Christmas" in a smarmy way is sure to create a problem at work. Wishing a Jehovah's Witness "Happy Birthday" produces a similar result. I'm not in favor of censorship, but avoiding religious discussions goes far towards keeping the peace at work.

Sexuality – I am a firm believer that someone's sexuality is a very private matter. If you're gay, trans, bi, or whatever you choose to claim, that's your business. Don't discuss it at work. Being a gay man has nothing to do with driving a forklift and pulling orders for shipment, so it has no business being a topic of discussion in the breakroom. It's not shameful, it's just no one's business. When you broadcast this topic, you're guaranteed to stir feelings of either empathy or anger, and all the politically correct remedies won't change the way people truly feel. It's not some dirty secret, but it's a private matter, just like whether someone got pregnant through natural means or by artificial insemination – it's no one's business.

You must have a filter on your mouth,

You must direct your crew to have a filter on their mouths.

Some people tell you things that you'd be willing to sell your soul in order to "unhear" it. It also robs you of brain cells.

Milking the clock and clock watchers

In 2003, while returning from Jersey City, New Jersey after testifying at a trial, I was buzzing down the New Jersey Turnpike on my way back to the Philadelphia area. It was around 3:00 pm on a Friday. I was running about 68 in a 65, and ended up behind a small box truck. An Isuzu, specifically, with a fourteen-foot box like you'd rent when moving. This one belonged to an electrical supply business out of southern New Jersey. The guy was driving much slower than the rest of us in traffic, going around forty miles an hour. It took a minute for traffic in the next lane to clear before I could get around him, and as I passed him, I noted it was two young men in their twenties, kicked back and relaxing on a leisurely drive. For anyone who has driven on the New Jersey Turnpike, you know there's usually nothing leisurely about it.

A few miles later, I dropped into one of the turnpike service plazas for a restroom break and a drink. As I walked out to my car, the two guys in the electrical supply truck pulled up next to me. I gave them the usual head nod as the driver got out. I had to ask why they were going so slow.

Me: "Dude, I almost ran into you. You're driving like an old man," I said with a laugh.
Dude: "Yeah, well, it's Friday, and I'm not hurrying back to the shop for shit, know what I mean?"

Me: "Not really, I'm self-employed. What do you mean?"

Dude: "Shit, we get back early, the damned boss would just have us go back out and deliver something else. I'll roll up there at five minutes to five and clock out and go home."

Me: "How far you got to go?"

Dude: "Nothing but twenty miles. We're gonna hang out here until about 4:30."

Me: "Alright, have a good one."

By the way, it was 3:15.

Folks, this kind of thing happens every day. People "milk the clock" on their employers. Sometimes it's hard to detect, sometimes it's very easy. In 2003, we didn't have Google maps on our phones, but we do now. What I'm saying is that if you were the manager for these guys, you could pull up their route, check it frequently, and turn on the "traffic" selection that shows you slowdown areas. If you note no significant traffic issues, but it took them three hours to make a one-hour run, you have some very valid questions that need answers.

Breakfast burritos - I managed a company a while back that engaged in heavy truck towing and repair. The shop manager opened the shop at 7:30 am, but the breakfast burrito truck would arrive right at that time. The shop crew would buy breakfast, and then stand around shooting the breeze for thirty minutes, and not even touch a tool or a truck until at least 8:00 am. This particular manager was fairly weak and didn't like confrontation, but I explained that the solution was easy. If the guys want to come in and have a "BS" session every morning, that's fine. They don't get paid until they pick up a wrench and a work order. This shop had five guys milking at least thirty minutes a day. The average guy made $18.00 an hour. With your 1.4 quotient, that's $25.20 per hour. Divided by two, representing the thirty minutes, that's $12.60, and times five guys is $63.00.

The manager was paying his crew $315.00 a week to stand around, shoot the breeze, and eat breakfast burritos. That's $16,380.00 in lost revenue in a year.

Shortcuts are also a revenue killer. Most employees and some managers believe that shortcuts save them time and make them money, but in the long run, you may find a different answer.

In 2000-2001, Chrysler had a huge recall on Dodge Neon head gaskets. Bear with me, this is technical, but I'm sure you can apply it to something in your business.

A good friend was the new shop foreman and the now-closed Chrysler/Plymouth/Jeep/Dodge dealer in Goldsboro, North Carolina, and one of young technicians devised a short cut to get through these low-paying (warranty labor rate) recall jobs quicker.

My friend joined the dealership just in time to reap the aftermath of this shortcut method.

In short, the cylinder head is removed and sent out to a machine shop to check tolerances and condition, and usually the surface that mates to the engine block is machined and cleaned up. The technician then reinstalls the cylinder head with a new head gasket kit and bolts it all back together. The labor operation only paid about four hours, so this technician figured out a way to unbolt the head, pry it upward a few inches, but not disconnect anything else – none of the wires, hoses or lines. He then took a ping-pong paddle and attached a razor scraper to it, and scraped at the mating surface to try to clean it a bit. He would then slip in the new gasket and bolt everything back together. He could do the job in an hour and was paid for four hours.

This sounds great until you own one of these "short-cutted" cars. The cylinder head, in his method, was never removed and inspected. It wasn't sent out to the machine hop to be checked using serious instruments. The cylinder head surface wasn't machined and perfect. The engine block surface wasn't even cleaned well.

My friend estimated that the young guy had done about twenty of these jobs in his manner, and *eighteen of them returned with leaking head gaskets, overheating cars, and in two cases, engine failures*. Angry customers, calls to Chrysler corporate, the technician was fired, the service manager was fired...all because some lazy guy wanted to save time and effort.

Shortcuts in fields dealing with heavy equipment, towing and recovery, trucking, and others can be dangerous and can kill people. You then have lawsuits, lost time, and businesses going out of business. It's not worth it.

"Clock watchers" are a special category. They watch the clock like a hawk, making sure you're not getting a moment or a second extra of their time, and you can see them planning their bolt out the door for up to an hour before normal quitting time. Their desks are arranged for the next day, and they shoot the breeze with other coworkers, take several restroom or smoke breaks, or find reasons to leave early or arrive late. It seems there's always something going on in their personal lives that means they must leave early. Especially on Friday.

Hourly employee apathy – I can tell, just by the way someone moves at work, whether they're paid hourly or by salary, or if they have an ownership stake in the company. These mannerisms go way back, and there is even more of a separation in recent years. I'm generalizing, as not all hourly works are apathetic, and not all owners are "nose to the grindstone."

Like the ones milking the clock away from the jobsite, these folks usually find menial, time-consuming tasks to keep them busy, or to appear busy. They may take an hour to sweep and mop an area that other employees clean in less than half that time.

You'll see them at a convenience store or truck stop, and they're out gathering trash bags from the containers, but they're also smoking, playing on their phones, or engaging in random conversations. While it may seem picayune to point this out, they're being paid to work, and if they're not actually working – or if they're dragging out a task – you're losing revenue.

If an hourly employee who makes $12.50 an hour "screws off" for two hours per day, and trust me, that's easy to do, you're looking at an actual cost of $35.00 ($12.50 x 1.4 x 2 hours) per day. That's $175.00 per week, and $9,100.00 in a year.

Other methods of apathy just involve laziness and neglect. Again, I'm using the convenience store or truck stop employee as an example, and things like not stocking or resupplying cups, lids, and straws makes for angry customers. Not stocking toilet paper and paper towels in the bathrooms makes for *really* angry customers.

These notions can be applied to many areas in any service-related business.

Many people in hourly positions have checklists to accomplish during their shifts, and again, I reference a convenience store. There's stocking, fronting products on shelves, sweeping and mopping, taking out trash, etc.

Through complaining, bitching, whining, and gossiping, people spend more time and energy trying to get out of work than if they'd just done their job. Not that I'd recommend allowing a bunch of "screw off" time, but if the employee just ran their checklist and accomplished their tasks, they'd likely find that they would have quite a bit of time left over in their shift. They're working *harder and longer* by trying to get out of work than if they'd just do the job in the first place.

"Calling out" – If there's one thing in the employment sector that truly gets to me, it's people "calling out" or "calling off" of work. As an employer, if you allow this for any reason other than something serious, you're setting yourself up for failure.

In many interviews I've conducted, I often ask a specific question about calling in to get out of a shift. I ask if the person, in a previous position, has ever called in to the boss and gave them whatever reason (illness, no babysitter, car is out of gas, monkeys escaped from the zoo)…to get out of work for that day.

I'm not referring to planned time off or serious family emergencies – I'm talking about last-minute call-ins where the employee won't be showing up that day.

Depending on the answer, eye contact, non-verbal movements, and other indicators I get after that question, I go on to explain the only valid reasons why someone could "call out" and still expect to have a job.

Those are:

My wife (or I) is/am having a baby.

My mom/dad/child/grandparent died. And keep track, because I've had people use the grandparent thing four times.

My house is on fire.

I was, or my immediate family member was, in a serious car accident and I'm in the hospital.

Any other absence needs to be covered with paperwork from a doctor's visit.

My methods seem harsh, and yes, you can relax these ideas after someone is hired if they prove to be generally reliable, but watching for the eye contact and other non-verbal reactions while going over these points yields priceless employer information. The concept is to create an environment where "calling out" simply isn't an option.

The "Star" Temp Worker

I kept this one out for last, and wanted it to have its own chapter, mainly because it still boggles my mind.

While I was in the Air Force Reserve, I took a position as a shipping and receiving manager for a large home improvement chain store in South Texas. I regularly did troubleshooting work in other departments at the behest of the store manager, and we were going to be doing a large-scale store reset soon and a big inspection team was coming in from corporate. There had been quite a lot of old boxes, some appliances, pallets, and other things that weren't really trash that were behind the store. The manager wanted it all gone, and tasked me with supervising a ten-person crew we'd hired through a staffing agency in Houston. I was to get the crew to clean everything up and have our delivery guys take loads of stuff to the nearby landfill. I had three days. Easy enough.

The staffing agency's vans dropped everyone off on the first day, and I had an even mix – five men and five women. As I talked to and worked with each one, I noted several personality styles, and worked with them to assign tasks that suited their styles. One guy was pretty rowdy and had a lot of energy. I assigned him to running the chain saw to cut through pallets and other wood scraps. The landfill has size requirements for the pieces of wood they'd take, and we had to cut some items to fit.

One guy showed up with hiking boots and a Camelbak hydration backpack. I assigned him and a very fit lady to picking items up around the store's perimeter fence and parking lot.

Others sorted stock items that needed to be returned to their departments. One guy loved sweeping and mopping, for whatever reason.

One guy, though, we'll call him Maurice, was never to be found when I would look for him. He would magically appear at lunch break and when it was time to go home, but was very difficult to find during the day.

I'll explain his unique qualities in the letter of recommendation he asked me to write for him. He told me that he had been at the staffing agency for quite some time, and there was this one great job he truly wanted. He needed a letter of recommendation from a work supervisor to get him in the door. I obliged.

Please peruse the letter:

(Name of store)
200 Hwy 332 East
Lake Jackson, Texas 77566

(Name of staffing agency)
Houston, Texas
July 22, 1999

Dear staffing agency manager,

It has been my pleasure to work with your staffing agency in filling a need we had for additional labor help. You sent the requested ten representatives from your agency. Maurice Smith was also assigned to this team along with nine others from your agency to help our store with a massive clean-up operation. Maurice Smith requested that I write a recommendation letter for him, as he is trying to gain a temp-to-hire position through your company.

The other nine people worked flawlessly and should be commended. Maurice, however, stood head and shoulders above his contemporaries, and demonstrated some incredibly gifted talents. Talents like I have only seen in the military, or on game shows. Please allow me to explain.

Maurice has an astonishing quality involving stealth. Stealth of movement, of sound, of presence. It's as if he's not even in the room or in the building. I haven't seen stealth like this since I worked with Navy SEALS, Army Rangers, or members of a SWAT team. One of my favorite characters, the Invisible Man from the Marvel Universe of superheroes, possesses similar skills. Maybe Maurice has super powers.

Maurice has an ability to acquire information that would make an FBI Director or foreign government spy proud. In less than three days, he acquired the names, phone numbers, and marital status of at least six of our ten dayshift female cashiers and customer service workers.

Maurice possesses the character and negotiating skills only rivaled by the famous Tom Sawyer from Mark Twain's book. When he was present, in the room, visible, and available for work, he could trick or guilt the other staffing agency workers into doing work for him. Unlike Tom Sawyer, I doubt that he went down to the river to fish, but I know he made several trips to the nearby Dairy Queen to purchase milkshakes (during work hours, not on breaks). According to the Dairy Queen manager, he was a very personable guy who asked several of his female employees out on dates.

Maurice is one of the most resourceful people I've ever met. I'd say that he's one of the most resourceful people I've ever worked with, but even though he was assigned directly to me and my store, he and I never actually worked together.

I wish him good luck and Godspeed in whatever path he chooses.

James E. Lewis
Shipping and Receiving Manager

The following Monday, I got a call from the staffing agency manager. She related that she'd passed my letter around to all of their eleven branches, everyone had a good laugh...and Maurice was no longer with them.

Solutions

This isn't going to be easy. You're going to have to get more involved and stay involved. You're going to have to change the way you interview, how you advertise positions, and before all of that, you need to get with your HR department and let them know you're changing things up. If you're a manager, I suggest getting your supervisor involved before initiating a different style of leadership and accountability. Use these methods as a trial, perhaps.

I can imagine the employees who have been with you the longest will be the hardest to reach and will take the most time. New hires can meet the "new you" easily enough during the interview and orientation processes. As you add to your staff, and perhaps "cull the herd" somewhat, you can install a new generation of people who are on your page of music.

As you may be able to tell, I'm pretty intense. People expect a lot out of me, and I expect a lot out of others. That's why I try to communicate so completely and technically. You must communicate with people if you expect them to act or perform a certain way. No one can read your mind. You don't have the right to be offended, angry, or upset if a person does something you don't like...when you never spelled out your expectations in the first place.

Bad day? – before you get started, ask yourself if you're having a bad day, and might take it out on an employee. Also, think about the possibility that an employee is having a bad day.

THEN, further quantify it, and ask yourself (and the employee), are you having a bad day, or **did you have a bad five minutes and you're just milking it all day?**

Although this book is copyrighted, the general methods of what I'm going to pass out aren't any sort of secret. A little old-fashioned, perhaps, but not a secret. I'm saying it's time that we bring some old-fashioned accountability, work ethic, character, honor, and pride back into our jobs and workplaces.

If you were hiring me to come into your business and set up this new program, and we worked side-by-side, there are several steps I'd advise for us to take.

Overall evaluation – check out and document your impressions on smoke breaks, gossip time, negative discussion time, and other distractions.

One-on-one meetings – Making big changes without some times and lots of communication could be a disaster. People are naturally resistant to change.

How you set up your new program, or way of doing things needs to be tailored to your own personality and leadership style.

One-on-one meetings are a great way to go over the basic programs, and get individual input. During these meetings, I've found people to be very positive. It's when they return to their work centers and begin discussing things with their coworkers that the sparks may begin to fly. After all, you're asking some of them to completely change the way they talk. Their actual language.

Group meetings – keep these meetings light, but to-the-point and firm. Do some math before you begin, and express the revenue losses in real dollars, and give examples of where that money could be better spent or used.

Discuss with the group(s) the negative and positive health impacts of being either negative or positive in your words and actions.
Discuss how easily a quick five-minute conversation can turn into an hour of gossiping, and again explain what that costs the company.

Bullies/Queen Bees/Mood Swingers – I listed this first because these people are the #1 cause for most people leaving a job. They're also the #1 cause of stress, anger, and apathy in the people that decide to stay with you.

As I stated before, a bully may project his/her own feelings of vulnerability onto the target(s) of the bullying activity. Despite the fact that a bully's typically denigrating activities are aimed at the bully's targets, the true source of such negativity is ultimately almost always found in the bully's own sense of personal insecurity and/or vulnerability.

In my mind and experience, there are only two ways to deal with a bully or Queen Bee:

1) Recognize that the bully is insecure, and without getting overly personal, try to discover their insecurity, and work to rehabilitate it.

    Understand that these people have worked very hard to hide their insecurities, and project a tough, mean exterior. Without significant work, you may not be able to crack their outer shell and help them improve. The end game is to work with them to heal the problem, while substantially fortifying their strengths and abilities, thereby making their insecurities much less important and impactful on their daily behavior.

2) Bullies and Queen Bee types want to play a hard role and project that tough exterior, and you'll have to be tougher. If you can't reason with them, the old adage of

"my way or the highway" may come into play. YOU are the manager/owner and this person is likely having a devastating impact on your business. Protect yourself accordingly.

Revise your interviews – the interview process is the perfect opportunity to gauge a person's negative or positive personality. You can ask unusual but simple questions, and even though they're putting their best foot forward, their answers may surprise you. Unique questions like:

Have you ever had a coworker bring gossip to you? What was your response?

Have you ever had a coworker who was always negative or in a bad mood? How did you work with them?

*** Have you ever had a boss or manager with an authority complex? (This one will give you insight on their acceptance of authority, or if their authority was challenged by the manager, you might discover how they reacted to that)

Have you ever had to call out of work? For what reason? (Perhaps go into your personal policy on the subject)

Have you ever suspected a coworker of calling out without a valid reason, or giving an outright false reason? How did you handle that? (I've asked...did the coworker ask you to lie or cover for them? This question goes a long way towards discovering morals, ethics, and character)

Hourly employee apathy – You should to tread lightly here, as less mature people will assume you're saying they aren't doing their jobs. There's a good chance that many aren't doing their jobs - not to the fullest extent, at least, and the company isn't getting their money's worth out of the employee. That's hard to say and even harder to take, but when an employee "screws off", spending time gossiping, shooting the breeze, playing on their phone, horse playing, or other non-work-related conduct, it does cost the company revenue. An employee is hired to come to work and do a job for their allotted shift, not spend two hours a day BSing with their buddies.

Cell phone policy – my oldest son works as an electronic and hydraulic technician as a huge distribution center. The folks there had a problem with distracted employees always playing on their phones, but it calls, texting, Facebook, games, whatever.

The resolution was simple. Phones stay in their lockers except on breaks and during lunch. Period. In this huge distribution center with eighteen miles of conveyors and more than four thousand machines to deal with, per-unit productivity on routine maintenance procedures increased by over 30% after the phone "ban."

It's your place of work. Phones aren't a necessity in most jobs – in fact, they're a significant distraction. And my son says he really doesn't miss his phone, and checking for updates gives him something to do during lunch.

Work assignments – we all know those employees I like to refer to as "forty-year-old adolescents." They may physically BE forty, but their conduct and maturity level are stuck on twelve. A grown man who will throw a tantrum over some trivial or petty work issue that reminds you of a pissed off twelve-year-old girl who just told she couldn't meet her friends at the mall.

Evaluate your crew - Every day. Know who your twelve-year-olds are. Separate them from other twelve-year-olds. Assign them with a true adult team leader. You can imagine that assigning two twelve-year-olds to the same task, especially if working away from the rest of your crew or your work location, would result in horse play and accountability problems.

Counseling sessions – the issue that most people in leadership positions face is lack of training or experience. Your supervisor didn't teach you how to be a leader, usually because no one taught them. When you witness negative behavior, be it complaining, gossiping, apathy, or general screwing off, you must nip it in the bud. Call an immediate counseling session with the employee and get straight to the point.

Follow up any communication or counseling session with written documentation. Why? Try firing an employee with no documentation. Even in states with "at-will" employment, most business owners and HR managers want a thick file of documentation to protect them in case of a lawsuit, unemployment filing, or fraudulent worker's comp claim. Protect yourself. This can be simple as an email to yourself, with a courtesy copy to your boss, indicating you spoke to the employee on a particular subject, and show the results or assumed outcome of the meeting.

This should be more formal in orientation or training scenarios, were documentation is expected. Lay it all out on the table, stick to your guns, correct and counsel when they're wrong, and document to cover yourself. It's an easy cycle to follow, and one that will protect you, your business, and your position.

Complaint jar – I know it seems silly, but many offices and homes have a "swear jar" where you have to drop in a dollar if your let a curse word fly. Why not institute a "complaint jar", or use "whine" or "cry" depending on the sense of humor and sensitivity of your employees?

When employees hold other employees accountable, positive behavior is rewarded and negative behavior is brought out in a big way – every gets on board, and it's like a game.

Joe walks into the accounting department complaining about the weather. Make him pay a dollar. Each section could have a jar, and the money collected could be used to buy donuts on Friday for the section doing the collecting, not the ones complaining.

Monday Blues – It commonly takes several hours to get people into their daily routines when coming back from a weekend. People feel the need to compare notes about their weekend activities, share gossip, and complain that it's Monday again and that they have to be at work.

Observe your crew and see who the polarizing figures are – the ones who instigate these conversations and activities. Assign them tasks first thing on Monday. Hold a meeting at 8:05 when your business opened at 8:00. Take charge, assign tasks, but most importantly, recognize the good work of select people or sections and show sincere gratitude. Walk them through the Monday Blues with an upbeat meeting and make it a subject that no longer causes a complete work stoppage for the first few hours of a week. Do the math, compare wages (times 1.4), and the time it takes it get people going on their own, and see what the Monday Blues are actually costing you.

Friday Fever – Fridays are the opposite of Mondays, for apparent reasons, but it's quite common to lose your crew for most of Friday afternoon as they contemplate their weekend activities. Discussions of visiting relatives, BBQs, football games, and karaoke night at the local bar can take a few of your good people and wrap them into several hours of wasted time.

Again, do the math and see what Friday Fever costs you. Plan a group discussion for Friday morning to talk about what each person has planned for the weekend, if it's not too personal. That takes the wind out of their sails for Friday afternoon, as they've already discussed the subject in a brief, controlled manner. Then "line them out" (assign tasks, make sure they have everything they need) for the rest of the day and you may have eliminated Friday Fever from your workplace.

Public Information – Tailor this to your specific workplace and business, as well as your personality style. Post information on a bulletin board or internal company website about wasted time and the cost to the company…and how their wasted time keeps them from getting raises, bonuses, BBQs, etc. Explain some of the staggering costs that I've given you the math formulas to calculate, and break down the things you could do for the business and staff if you could reduce this wasted time.

And remember - revenue is revenue, no matter where it comes from.

One last thing – **It is what it is**.

I lived near Philadelphia for several years and heard this phrase all the time. It drove me crazy, if you can imagine Rocky Balboa saying "Hey, it is what it is."

I finally got the chance to ask a mentor-type about the phrase, one of my education managers at the technical school where I taught – older Italian guy, hard accent, and dropped "It is what it is" at least twenty times a day. I demanded to know what it *meant*. The way he laid it out made perfect sense, and ties into the lessons I've dropped into this book.

It is what it is. No matter how a particular situation is handed to you, what condition you receive a problem in, how you're told a story, or given a piece of equipment, it is what it is.

You have no control over the issue, piece of equipment, or scenario before you get it.

You can do one of three things with "it" when it is presented to you:

1) Do nothing. Drop the ball. Ignore it. Hope it goes away. *And it won't.* Ignoring a problem or broken piece of equipment does nothing but kick the proverbial can down the road.
2) You can make it worse. You can overreact. You can freak out. You can delegate it to someone who doesn't know anything about it. You can draw attention to your unit or section and make sure the big boss knows you and your section don't know what you're doing.
3) You can fix it. Research, evaluate, study, use common sense and experience and make "it" better, whatever "it" is.

As you can see, there's only one way to deal with "it" successfully.

And remember – it is what it is. Handle it.

And revenue is revenue.

I can be reached at james@roninmotivation.com.

Feel free to contact me for workshops, advice, or strategic planning. I hold seminars nationwide, and I am available for audits and consulting.

www.ingramcontent.com/pod-product-compliance
Lightning Source LLC
Chambersburg PA
CBHW060351190526
45169CB00002B/563